THE SECOND
Garfield
TREASURY

THE SECOND Garfield TREASURY

JIM DAVIS

BALLANTINE BOOKS • NEW YORK

Copyright © 1983 by United Feature Syndicate, Inc.

The Sunday strips appearing here in color were previously included in black and white in *GARFIELD Weighs In, GARFIELD Takes the Cake, GARFIELD Eats His Heart Out, and GARFIELD Sits Around the House.*

All rights reserved under International and Pan-American Copyright Conventions. Published in the United States by Ballantine Books, a division of Random House, Inc., New York, and simultaneously in Canada by Random House of Canada Limited, Toronto.

Library of Congress Catalog Card Number: 83-90071

ISBN 0-345-31225-2

Manufactured in the United States of America

Designed by Gene Siegel

First Edition: November 1983

10   9   8   7   6   5   4   3   2   1

This book is dedicated to the cartoonists whose strips were in the Marion Chronicle-Tribune, Marion, Indiana, in the early '50s. They were the ones who inspired me to become a cartoonist and influenced my philosophy of cartooning.

This book is dedicated to: Sparky Schulz (Peanuts), who proved there is humor in the gentle things in life; Milton Caniff (Steve Canyon), who whisked me away to exotic places I never dreamed existed; Mort Walker (Beetle Bailey), whose every line and every word was distilled into pure humor; Hal Foster and John Cullen Murphy (Prince Valiant), who set an artistic standard that will never be matched again; Chic Young (Blondie), who taught me the value of interpersonal relationships in a strip; and Walt Kelly (Pogo), who carved a niche on the comics page for true creative genius.

This book is dedicated to my mentors...my friends.

JIM DAVIS

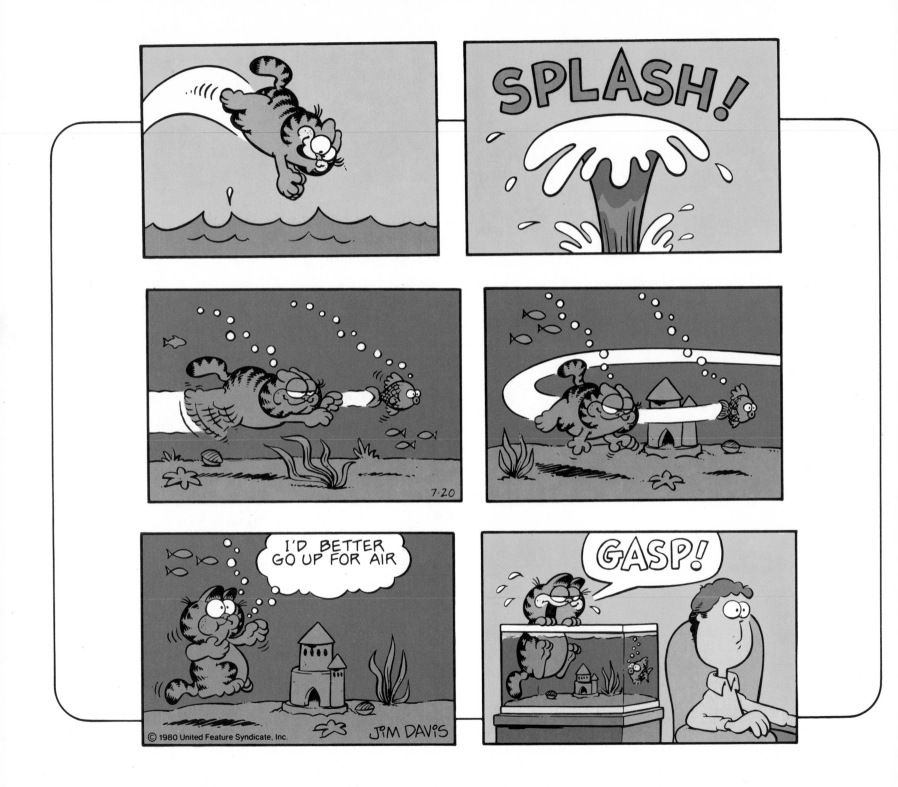

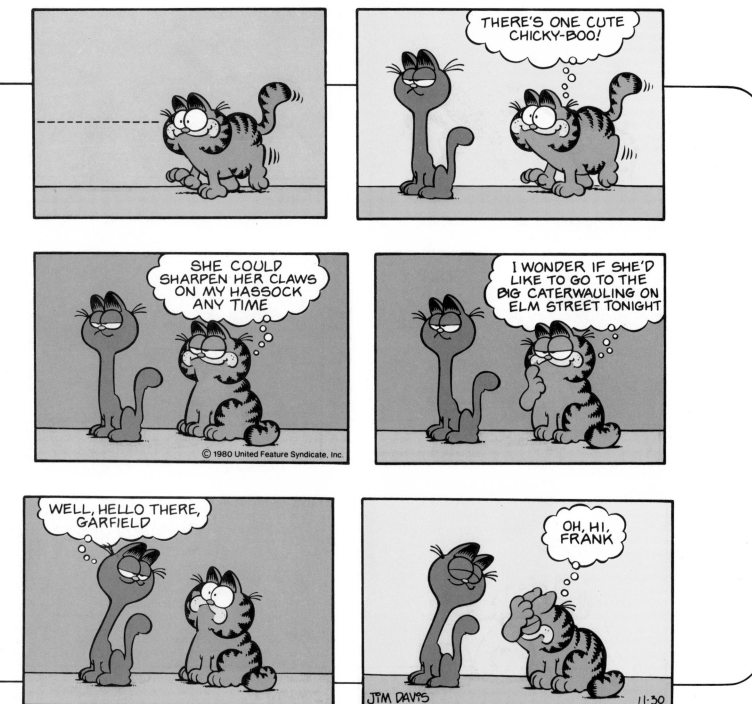

JIM DAVIS

2-8

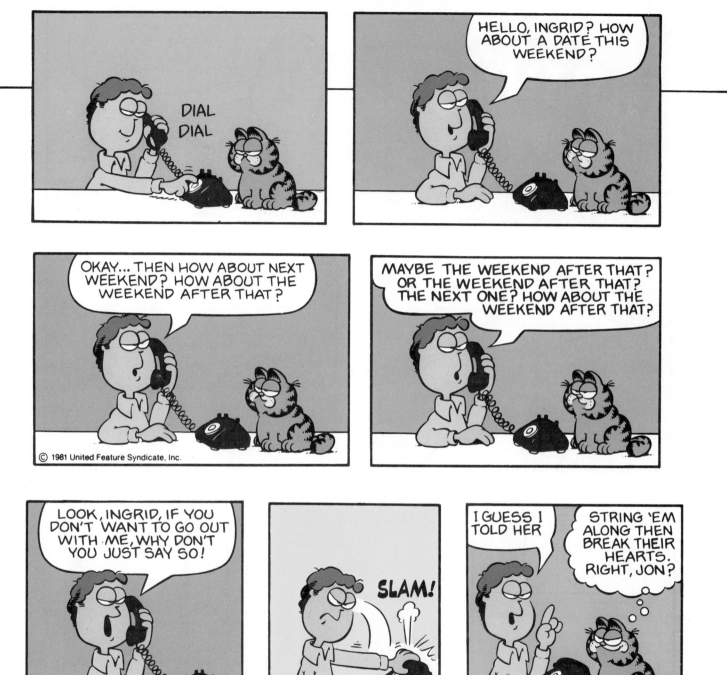

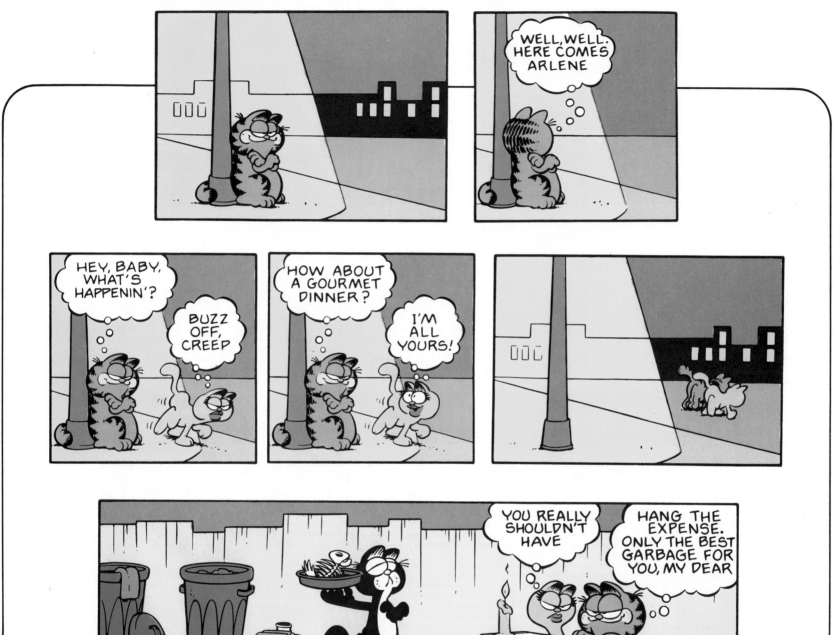

JiM DAViS

7-5

OH YUK!

WHAT DID YOU DRAG THAT FISH IN FOR?

SMACK!

BONK!

WHEN A CAT PRESENTS YOU WITH A DEAD, SMELLY THING, IT'S AN EXPRESSION OF LOVE, YOU TWIT

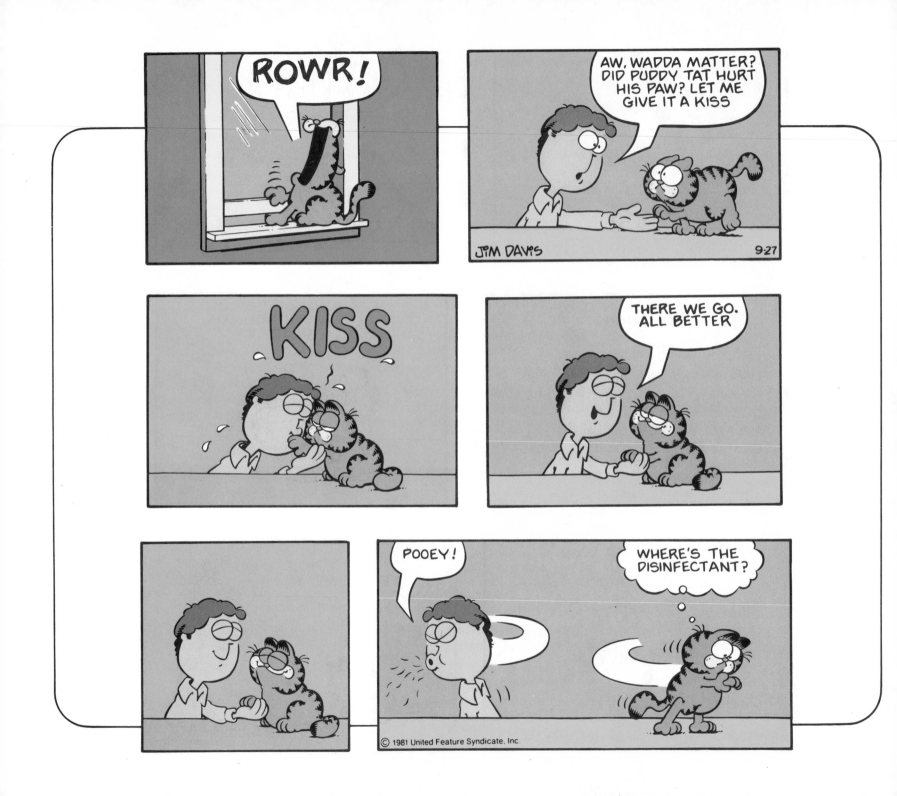

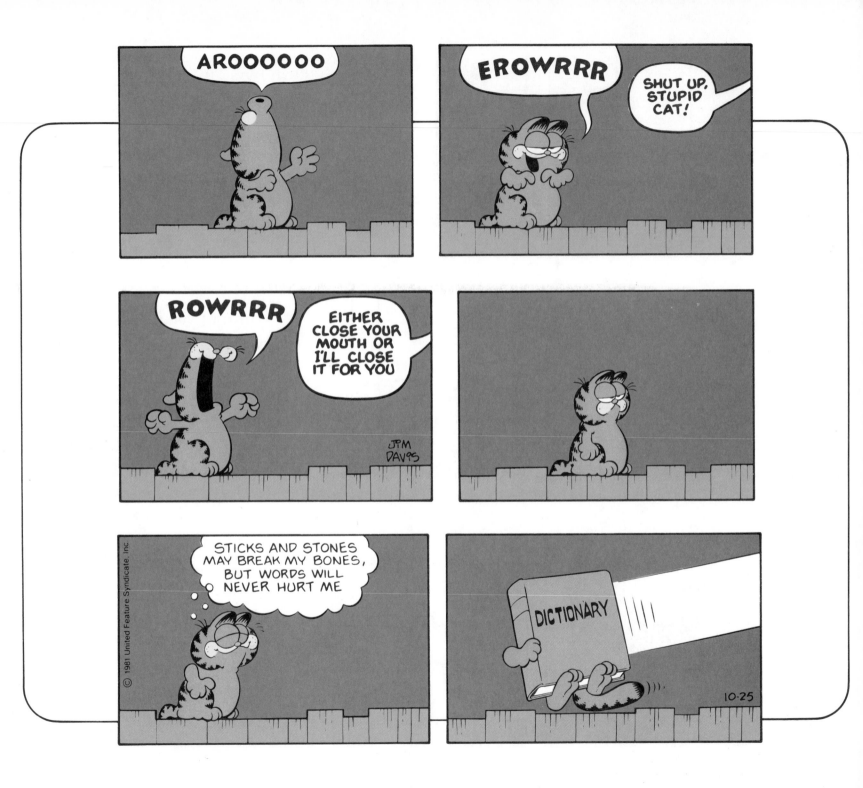

JIM DAVIS

11-22

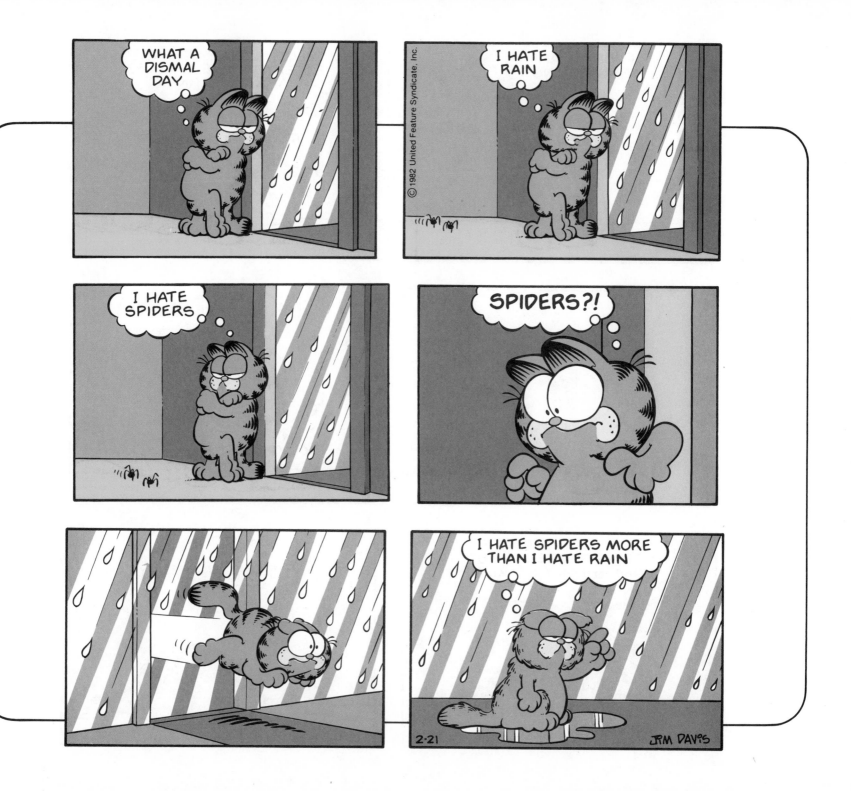

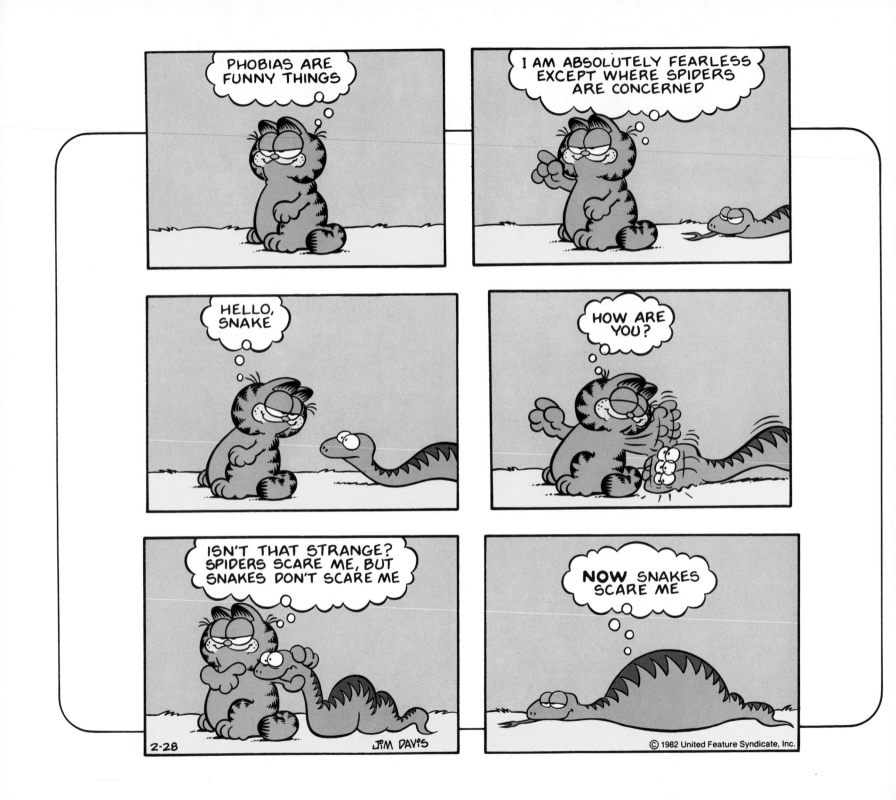

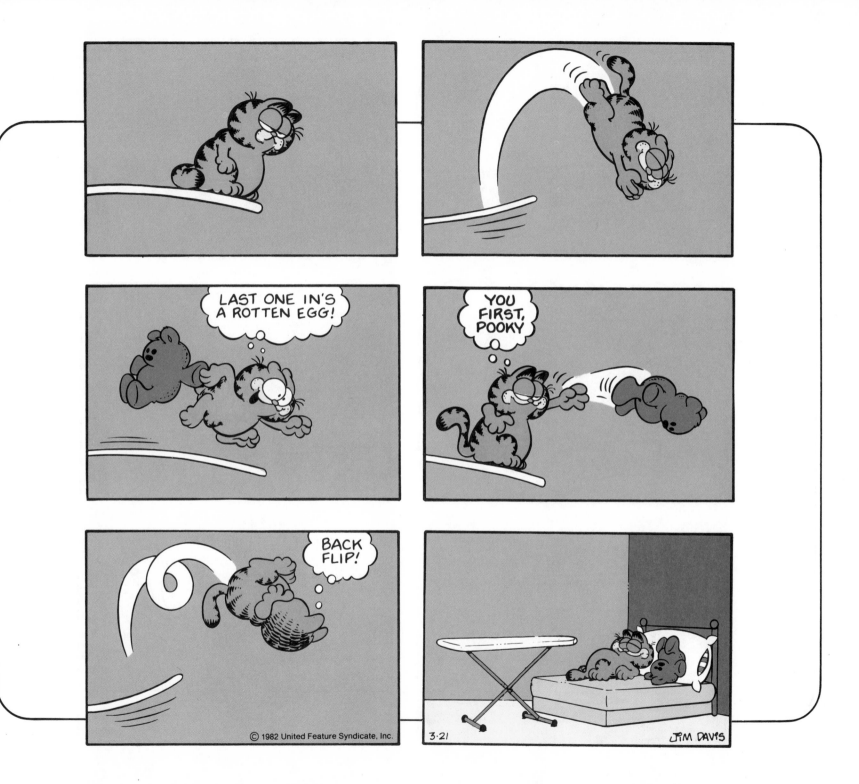

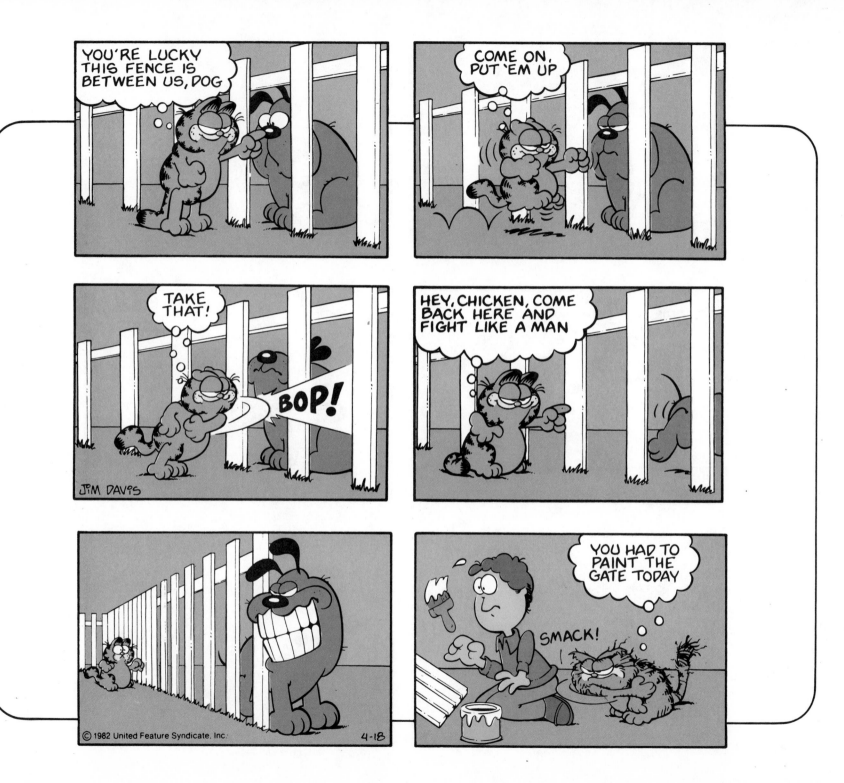

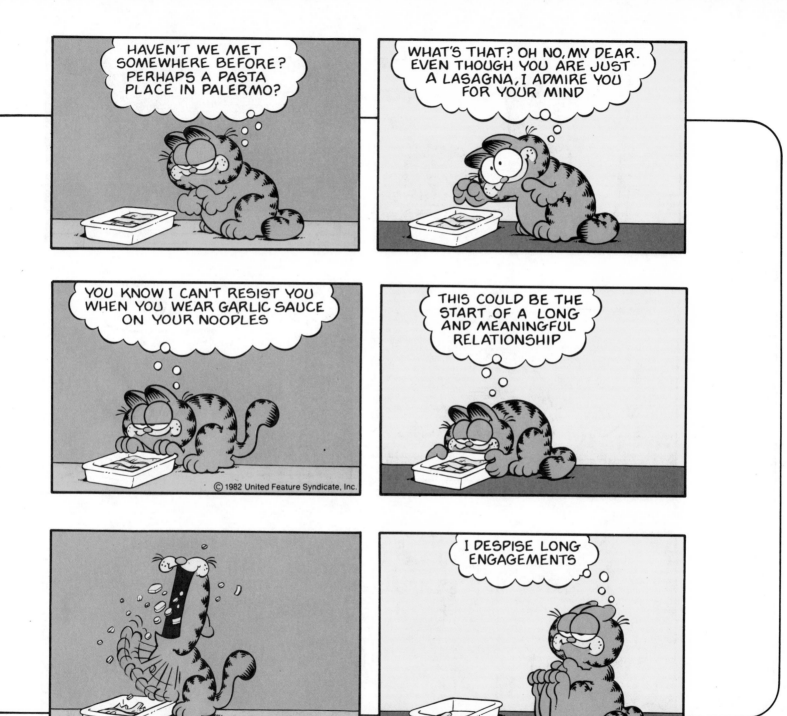

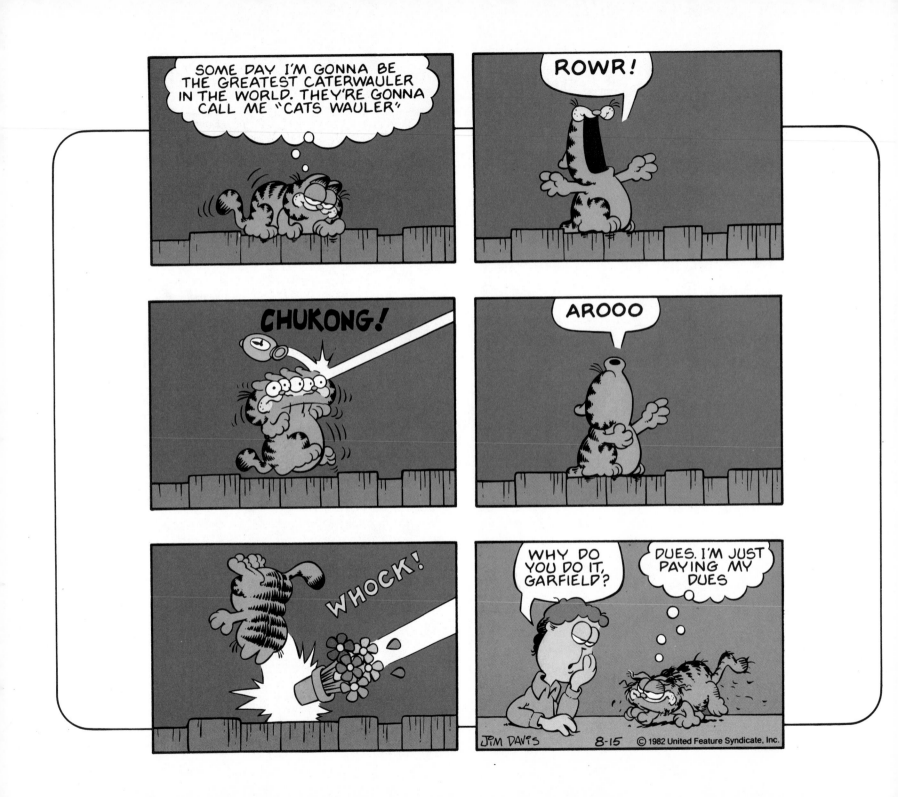

Find 10 things wrong with this picture.

6. Garfield's bed is made. 7. Nermal is holding Pooky. 8. Fern on fireplace is not destroyed. 9. Diet Tips book against Garfield's bed. 10. Arm of chair is not shredded.

ANSWERS: 1. Garfield is taking a bath. 2. Arlene is eating Garfield's food. 3. Odie is chasing mice. 4. Pan of lasagna uneaten. 5. Garfield isn't tripping Jon carrying the groceries.

JIM DAVIS

It may have been destined from the very beginning that Jim Davis would create Garfield. Jim grew up on a small farm in Fairmount, Indiana, surrounded by 25 cats. He was asthmatic as a child and was stuck indoors with his paper, pencil, and imagination to play with. It was the imagination that did it.

Jim attended Ball State University as an art and business major and received such honors as one of the lowest cumulative grade point ratios in the history of the university.

After college, Jim went to work for an advertising agency, during which time he met his wife Carolyn, a gifted alto with the Ball State University Singers. (It's been rumored that she tried to teach Jim to sing but gave up in defeat.)

In 1969, Jim started working with Tom Ryan on the syndicated comic strip "Tumbleweeds." Jim's first attempt at his own strip was "Gnorm the Gnat." Gnorm, however, went down in defeat. The syndicates felt it might be a little difficult for readers to relate to a bug.

After months of waiting for that all-important decision, Garfield was accepted in January of 1978 by United Feature Syndicate.

Paws, Inc., an art facility for all Garfield merchandising, is the only studio in existence for a licensed character. The Paws staff grew from three people to fifteen in one year's time.

The Garfield strip is now in over 1,400 papers, making it the fastest growing strip in history. Merchandising for Garfield is worldwide.

With all his success, Jim's favorite things in life are still simple—good friends and good food.